Strawberry Ashes

Lucy Medina

NEWMAN SPRINGS PUBLISHING
320 Broad Street
Red Bank, NJ 07701

First originally published by Newman Springs Publishing 2021

ISBN 978-1-63692-674-2 (Paperback)
ISBN 978-1-63692-675-9 (Digital)

Printed in the United States of America

To Linda Diaz—for always appreciating the little things

Strawberry Ashes

Kisses like strawberries sweet to an embrace of hunger and pain, I burn slowly for those who suffer with nothing left to bleed through but swollen veins. I stand in rain to soothe the burning, cursed with the gift of words that would trouble the sleep of the human in chains. My body disintegrating into sweet-smelling ashes. Open your senses with intent to imagine and scream my name, taste my strawberry ashes as I crumble apart to dust and blow away.

Yesterday's Tomorrow

Things of yesterday seem quiet. Listening to the sound of the cars go by seem, more distant and as if I know where they are headed. Seeing behind my eyes I feel as if I know now that all I've had for some time now will be swallowed by yesterday and tomorrow will be empty. Nothing left but the silhouette of what once had a home here. To lay my head seems needed but I don't know how to say goodbye and close my eyes…knowing when they open all that was beheld in front will be nothing but an empty space. The lesson is profound, the words dancing in my head are undefined, the heartache is real.

Undarkened Glasses

To Linda Diaz

Taking photo of my surroundings, discovering the beauty in God's subtle gentle touches. The air soft and dying I inhale the breath of this life and compress the outside cruelty. Almost like sheltered in a pocket filled with autumn leaves and seasonal flowers just made for my eyes today. Scented with ocean and nestled with rain. Can almost make you drift into sleep to dream the beautiful dreams we subconsciously spend our whole lives to manifest. Like shade on sun perfectly breezed while blooming the reality that beauty is that peace we truly seek within the race of time here. Controlled and brutal, we remember the pains but forget the pockets of peace we are given, seeking guide the significant thought of feeling alone seeps out the skin like sweat. All around is company, in every living thing surrounding the beautiful camouflage we so often blind the eye to.

Devil's Dance

Subliminal messages in my subconscious. Bloody hands in my visions giving me the capability to give up give in, and the mundane takes a backward seat on my conscious blinded mind. No one sees the depth of it nor I but deep within myself. Skin and bone claw its way out and show the side of me that dances with the devil. And God one day will remind me not only whom my partner was in this dance, but down to detail of the song we danced to.

The Red Root

Anger, birthed from resentment. Uncontrolled, deep and dark, almost violent and bloody. Stepping back, the ghost of me sees but understands where the hate comes from.

A Woman's Sword

Feeling idle on this path, I'm on at this time in my life. Love was something I had but lost when it was meant to feel lasted. Afraid to act like what I had was love when in its entirety it was not. Left it to God, and angels whispered in my ears at night telling the story of a woman much like myself, who walked away to the unknown. But with courage and faith in that the love she desires exists in the cruelty of the world. I took a chance where I thought it mattered, broke my own rules to meet love halfway…Now feel bitten by the monster's teeth and clawed by the hands of a man I know little of. I will not carry it nor ignore it, but I will remember what I can take and give… And oh, how I have more to give. I have learned many lessons, given many thoughts to where I should or when I should lay my sword down. But I cannot lay it just anywhere. It needs to be put up high, passed a glancing eye so to remember the fight that lead me where I stand. Where I lay my head at night. Whether it be in your arms or beside you. If my sword is to be displayed standing alone, then I will do so with honor, humbled by my ability to do so.

Narrator's Lullabies

Sometimes the look in her eyes can tell him a story of an end. Whether that story is long or short depends on his perspective. She can probably choose to light the darkness behind his eyes. She can stand close by or choose to put space between distance. She reminds him of who he was. But because of her, he's proud of who he is now. During this story, her as the narrator speaking in the distance between the spaces…she can put beauty within the smallest of moments. She can add significance to his words, his silence, his kindness and his cruelty. She can offer him peace now, he can feel it…she knows. But she does not have the privilege of peace within herself.

The Light Hidden in the Light

In position to navigate and or review my life, I've taken note of things and those things done. In light I see beauty but with less obviousness, in dark I also see beauty with obsession. But obsession in ways of looking through cracks left on walls that tend to always form around to create the dark. These cracks, as I call them, are little sight for sore eyes like my own. They are the beauty I speak of, the light in the light less, noticeable in light, but in dark its shine is profound and hungry.

In my mind, my heart, I believe God has hands behind me and all around me. I gather that thought and suddenly understand, that in my darkness he knows its depths. He knows the deepest of hurt in the darkness I can sometimes live in that in my light, he is that light. Behind my eyes is secret and the deepest of wounds. Before me was plan; it always had to hurt. But the wounds are only deeper because I am just a mortal human. I fall victim and criminal to my pain, and God is my judge. My Savior, my Maker, and my humanity's humility.

Lucy's Faith

A beautiful melody surrounded a tainted heart like a mirrored door taunting me, so sincerely sorry. The image was familiar; the glass was broken but untouched. Through all its broken pieces, there lived hope with unstoppable love. In that love was poison that kills the hope of tomorrow. A graveyard lay deep between the cracks, with my reflection kneeling down on withered black roses that lay beside a stone. I fell in sadness as her tears soaked into the inscription. It read, *Here lies Lucy's faith.*

Diary

For what I've concealed, I know the time has passed and wasted. Holding on to distant memories and those stories that can't be told, these thoughts control the outcome of the day. I predict their stares and judgement if I speak the words I've left unspoken, to tell the stories of past demons that leave me shamed onto those who walk a straight line. So I remain unnoticed, keep my secrets and call it poetry. They remain sealed in my closet of pages and become my mirror confessions that will someday lead to my own forgiveness.

The Empty

Life is going to teach me many lessons. My reactions tested and judge me with jury. I long for the days to empty the empty and widen the full. My heart craves for the peace to find home in me and decide to make its bed and stay for a while. I take pieces and place them in areas that seem to have space, but it only molds around the edges and creates a thicker seal against those walls…as if it is bottomless. It can never be at capacity. It is like a box within a box within a box. Nonetheless, I continue. I continue to place in the empty.

Lucy vs. Luz

Something takes a seat upfront and reminds me of my two sides. Granting entertainment to the one that hides in the shadows leaves me quite breathtakingly settled. Twisted silhouettes speaking to me through sight but nonetheless not impossible to see its full meaning. Day taken apart, stretched to weeks and doors shut windows open and eyes, unsure. *Steady*, I whisper to myself, *steady*. Feel the ground beneath my feet, steady my hands to remove the clench I have on things I cannot change and take ahold of the solid stone that will offer me my peace.

Save the Innocence

Standing still has still led me to a place where paths are visible. Counting the hours till I decide takes away option, although I'm familiar with the countless times. I could stand for everything I believe in. My moral still brushes against the edges of something sharp, calling out a name we're all familiar with crying my way out of sin. Wondering if the almighty hears the screaming from within. Thankful for my shell being filled with me by my God but waiting for gratitude from somewhere deeper inside me where I sometimes think soul has bone.

Is it softened due to them being broken by the time body has died. The devil on my shoulder, the angel even closer to my beating heart, I closed eyes to gain sense to recognize the importance of peace on the inside. I've danced with devil too many times, but I realized in every dance he was who led. So I ask to change not only the partner but the song and the dance. And in the end, I'll take my bow and whisper amen.

The Silent Storm

A constant swing of emotion, a rhythm of beat from the heart. It almost seems like it wants me to follow but mind plays its own instrument in this. Thoughts of you…what consumes my heart and mind curses me, my lips held tightly closed and my heart pulls the strings to keep me silent. To you, it's quiet. To me, it is so loud and shakes me like an earthquake breaking me. Taking me further away from you. I silently stay, pretending I'm whole. I want to hold you, but I need to be held. I want to stand close by, but I'm pushed away. My loyalty spoke, my time passed. My silence has stood still.

I Kissed the Sun

A different kind of fire in my eyes today, a burning so entitled. A tormented flame urging my eyelids to shut and engulf my skull in flames. An end to an old beheld definition on my world, a beginning to what may survive the heat surrounding the ashes left behind. Perhaps there's more living beneath the ashes. Breathing in the hope of it leaves me gasping for a gust of wind that may someday be born in my blazing storm.

Choice has always huddled together with hope, but hope withers like thirsty leaves on a morning dews dawn...oh, the moment where you taste the humidity on the tongue...thirst comes faster than the eyes can bring tears. The fire lasts longer, more profound than ever, more sense to why it burns deep so undisciplined...taming this fire will swallow the humanity. Expecting the wounds to unravel is my sanity.

The Past Lives

Release the time as if I held it in the palm of my hand. See the past through different eyes, but never takes away...never.

Anticipate a genuine smile or characterize myself differently. Only honesty in myself as a whole person, a whole woman, to keep what I am and what I've been until the tongue dries. There will always be words to say, words to define the intensity of memory, my past, my present, and my future. But to try would be a blessing to see who dares. New words to speak when it is no longer needed in my blood. The soul is absorbing the magnificent of what an icy hand can hold with the creativity of what the heart can diminish when something so thirsty, so dry, becomes the masterpiece of what sealed its fate.

Uncontrollable Actions

As I continue this journey, present or future, which is or isn't what mixes decisions to mistakenly make me hate the impressions that create the emotions that prevent me from going or even bluffing to avoid some confrontations when it's conversation that makes the decisions that continue to break me when I try to relate the arguments that prevent me 'cause I hate me when I can't take the break down that they gave me because they can't understand me, even if I gave the time to explain the problems that make me want to believe you but only 'cause it took two for the issue to come to the tragedy that made me angry. So if I hate, they would disgrace me and label me an enemy.

Sorrow Pie

1 tablespoon of sleepless nights
2 cups teardrops and wipes
½ cup of missing you
4 cups of loving you too
1 tablespoon of jealousy
½ cup of bandages
1 cup of black and blues
4 cups of salt to pour on my open wounds

Cook it on 350°F for 45 minutes or more. Serve it on a silver platter and wait for you at the door.

The Puppeteering Puppet

Uncovered lips have a place here. I recall the hours and days I chose to cover my words, but in ways no one can see the dance on my tongue. Almost like it had its own song, moved the tongue like the wind moves the dead leaves on the ground on an October night. I can seem speechless, almost shocked would be the expression in my eyes. But the mind, my mind takes note on everything done, said, seen. Silence has noise, the noise inside my head. That's when and how the demons come out to play. It's the silence that makes them eager to pull my veins, playing the melody in my head and masters the art of puppeteering.

The Accent of Love

What a beautiful thing to say that there is nothing more to come into being with certainty. How eagerly awaiting his eyes to see clearly that love is at the surface, but oh how blind the man's eyes seem to be…if just for a moment, if he could lend an ear to listen the realization would certainly be there. I would hold tight. I would reassure the same as it gives. How the truth speaks through your action. How its silence hurts, its distance hides behind his lie to be there, to care so coldly only difference has excuses.

My heart speaks many languages; it speaks in depth to space the love through time. It speaks in laughter to shine the light into darkened eyes, it speaks in riddle to entice your thirsty mind, it speaks with warmth to soothe you. But I have fallen victim to my own theory, that for who knows only warmth, who knows only to be forgiven is in desperate need of darkness and cold. So that its need and want in its losses can rise and light the fire to warm again. A privileged man can only learn to see beauty if he lives a day blind to the beautiful and deaf to the languages of love.

First Name Book Last Name Chapter 1

I'VE described myself as a book of sorts. My cover is hard and significantly rough around the edges. My introduction would read "in dedication to eyes who read me upon looking for more than just the puns and exciting paragraphs." This wouldn't be a first book nor a best seller, but a time between a heartbeat capable and a break where the eyes meet with the hearts last supple innocence.

It will tell a story of beautiful things that existed even through the thickest of days, taking into consideration the humanity of things. It would speak of devotions and love eating away the fruit of the consciousness that is now numb, how sweetness became bitter and angry. How would I begin? Once upon a time? One day? How about, right now this day this moment. No pictures in me, just words written out of wounds and all the commas, question marks, periods and pauses just made from the exhale/inhale of a moment.

Spaces Between Distance

I'VE sat in my head today. Music plays my voices, my words in melody with not a sound from my lips. I sing inside the sadness and hold it tight enough to steel you. But I welded the memory of you in my skin. I look at the one I lie beside, but my heart lives so far away. His laughter tries to give my face a smile, his love tries to warm my heart...but it's not here...I feel it, but it's not here. So I stumble. I fall in the face I see, but I can't show you. So I am comforted by the temporary replacement from reality. It makes me laugh at the obvious...

The Artist

The drive in the mind, the desire in the body. To consciously want and need to reach, to catch or build with such focus, such intricacies within. Soul feeding heart beating to every stroke of brush to create beauty for the eyes. Or perfection in the fingers of musicians to create rhythms in sounds to soothe their soul. A need, for taste of delicate but savory food made from hands of valued taste. Creativity, from a place that makes reason, desire, want, come to life.

Lay Burden Down

A cold raindrop on the skin used to wash away the thickness of a day, could be why I loved the rain so much...

Nowadays it seems to blacken the skin, like drops of water on lava.

Resentment trickles down my spine, but why do I keep those resented still? With a different look, with a different feel I see...my eyes don't hold dearly the same as before. I do not feel the substance that was once a special kind of rest. Things I remember dance around but not much care to what they mean, no bother to what once was. The mind and heart held in contempt for its laughter today.

Where did the humor come from? Maybe from the backward reflection or silhouette from that distance, or maybe it's the dancing above my head. I once believed that there was choice to mend into peace...I was misunderstood. I accept, I accept all and with no compassion for any loss. I do not need to be excused, nor do I wish for bandages. Let it breathe, let it bleed freely for my conscious mind to keep its barriers around my heart.

The Truth Lied Under You

A running thought took you away from me, an even truth brought you closer. I've let you go long ago, but I've torn apart my own heart to find you again. You, you destroyed it when its beat were strongest. You're a beautiful lie. I am a wonderfully tainted woman that you've created, an end of a love story with only river to drown and applause from the creator. Even through my lovely pain, I've created a place for your head, a place for your hand, a place for your pain, and a fortress for your heart. You're just a beautiful lie. Awaiting my end to tell the story of your truth, your end, my end.

Times Instrument

Consumed with the thought of time I place my hand on the hand of time, subtle whispers beg for the seconds before but tempered reality also cruel for balance. Hold on tight enough to stay on ground, concrete messages feels like stone can't even hold an image on this earth. Mother Nature can wash away that stone, take it deep beneath the earth and only resurfacing when the ground opens up to swallow and feed. If I stare hard enough, will I lose sight and gain sense? If I hold for too long, will it become heavier? If I cry long enough, will I drown? If I know how to swim, does that mean I should live in the ocean?

Between the Editor's Lines

Watching the clock hour by hour wondering how time will tell my story. To remember where my heart was a year ago, now sensing the pain as if it made a home here. I've always known that I can stay by you for what many may perceive as for too long, but something is magnetic, cold when I start to find warmth and fire when I need ice. I've learned you created a paragraph with your name spoken millions of times in my book. Nestled in the pages you're safe, burdened in the ink I lay asleep. One day I'll read the story as an editor, not as a character, and remember where you played many. I'll decide to write in theory and possibly essays based on it. Enter a character burdened by the true story, leaving a reader ready to critique where the words lay temporarily.

Transparent Symphonies

I can remember the name that held onto my lips, on the way out extended emphasis on the sentences that follow. It held the sense but kept the moisture evaporated. The trembling ground off the sound, invisible melody taking shape to claw. Let's call it the rain, recycling the sound of transparent symphonies hitting the ground just like the hunger in thunder plays harder. The break swallows me like wine, a drunken mind not so deserving for clarity, words start to break apart and spell out a different song a soul old and tainted truth beneath the lie.

Its strength of the instrument screaming on the inside where winds are born, I'd Christian my soul show it mercy the sounds from the storm dance off my bone. Let's call it the rain, recycling the sound of transparent symphonies hitting the ground just like the hunger in thunder plays harder. My lyrics compromised to harmonize the sounds of the rain, storm comes rumbling in, and strings sound like rusted gears. The piano still plays and slowly drifts into distance. It's quiet now on the inside; it bled through the storm played its beautiful music too. Let's call it the rain, recycling the sound of transparent symphonies hitting the ground.

The Film

The human imagination can place illusion into my heart; sometimes I wonder if what the imagination is can be the actual. Spinning out of my own mind at full and ending empty then back again. Always more uncertain of how it supposed to feel this time around, what can I strip away and what can I give a name. All the while sometimes things strip away on their own, but is it due to my lack of, lack of understanding and or selfishness in the amount of attention I give. I may wear the armor I built on my heart, but the truth stripped away the steel. I've grown enough to realize that I can't possibly have the privilege, the knowledge, to understand the whys or hows of it all… but with the understanding, the knowledge, of knowing that to be so. Shouldn't that offer some peace?

If I spent a day as my own mirror watching my thoughts watching my emotions as if presented in a theatre big screen, could I somehow disconnect and become opposite to me. I would see blind progress made in wrong courses through wrong choices, maybe while the truth I know returns in my dreams. I keep my eyes open as my life plays on the screen, watching everything I never saw but felt. I figured I should disappear into the distance but I turned to make certain, but I couldn't look away. I couldn't even blink if my eyes burned, like watching the devil fall to his knees and pray to God…it was unheard of, strange and seemed forbidden but felt as if it brought balance to a downhill path on an uphill battle.

An End, a New Beginning

I compare what I've lost to what I've gained, it is the mirror the liar. Notably significant.

These different tongues are too harsh to ask, removing the dependency of the fact that each line is becoming another stain on the lip, a dialect corrupt. To be idle I would hold on, to a concept, try to retain an idea as it shatters and dilutes the taste on my tongue. Knowing the words, I say the words I've said. I wear it like armor and things have caused me to remove it.

To recount every wordless day, it is an impressive acknowledgment that I've learned after too long…the selfishness of others and that I can in mind and heart erase and see the intricacy of the blank of the white. It's misinterpreted truth is comforting I've changed unnoticeably, I created in the mind the most ultimate example. A beaten silhouette in the distance has the status to justify the amount of unjustified pain hovering around me that has been paid.

Hollowed Victory

Hate and love tremble between the same inconsolable resentment and the hope to reconciliation that stand side by side and fight the same war. But nothing seems worthy, it would be a crime to turn the eye away from the silence of the nothing.

Love and hate hold hand in hand, across me lies a way out. With thorns along the walls and glass on the road. Recovering broken bone but seeping flesh, out of grasp to the loss of warmth artificial from my heart. Carry the undone with a camouflage heart and a long spear, and at that moment where I am lost and home has gone. I will take my body to my blade in the midst of the thunder. We've always known it would end this way...The echoes took my eyes and made me still as the walls should not have been rebuilt on the same foundation it had crumbled upon. Blown away by mother earths resented son

Silhouettes lost in vain for all done.

Prayer Nestled in a Kiss

Beautiful when sun kisses the earth, but still I wait for night to feel value of its worth, like sun burned skin to hold and leave the imprints from within. I crawled before I could stand now here I am on my knees again.

Selfishness has its place in my bed, but selflessness is what gives me rest. Closing my eyes with dreams of faith, encountering truths of familiar face. Today lead to yesterday's hour, the things I still remember, I bound this truth sealed pages all together, with a kiss enclosed in its letters.

Undefined

My mind is conscious enough to understand. I see the difference just by where words are placed. A lot has been said, and unsaid, but all that has felt worthless once had worth. It took apart the existence of something we all hold dear. Powerful is what it was. Had a thick coat, could've taken a hurricane had it ever encountered one. Still the softest brush of winds carried you away. You let go, knowing I was the rock to steady us in the strongest of winds. I know how the hand feels when it lets go its grasp. I can still feel the warmth of that ghost, but I can never forget the reminder of never had pressed my cheek against your hand. If my hand was made of clay, your impressions would define the edges of my fingertips.

Tonight

Trying to bring the lies to life in this song.
I know that love doesn't belong here in this time.
Love has no place where there is no home.
Call it what you like tonight tonight...just for tonight...
I don't have no lies to share no times to take away...nothing to keep you...stay.
Call it what you like tonight tonight...just for tonight.
It's too far too far to hold close enough.
Your light didn't shine bright for me you didn't light the way for me...

The Beautiful Lie-oness

Suffocating for what I remember and half the heart still lives there, washing my eyes with the tears have not pierced through to clean the filth of you. I am still within the nightmares, fighting for a dream. I will live within the first place and time-consuming pictures from your heart-eaten words. The breath I take still keeps my heart beating, but the air is thin and short inhaled, constant half-lived life within my shell. I'VE seen something in your eyes, but lust lies, I've seen love in your eyes a lasting memory, a death of sense. You spoke the story of us, and I fell within your fable. I was the lioness, and you queened me with no place as king.

Limbo

In the dark closed eyes take blinded steps that can't remember, clenched onto the fabric of my skin, remaining still to the room with spinning memories still moving.

Beyond my vision. Taking place so near an open space. My name echoed with no light and shadow is but a dying wish that so secretly cries for a candle blowing in the wind. My hands behind my body still afraid to reach out and find my way home. No more sacrifice, for I cannot see a hand reaching from the darkness. My screams echo so loudly here…realizing, the space had no walls.

The Inspiring Beast

Hate can cloud around the winds blowing against my windows, the windows I call my eyes. I can see it faceless growling in anger to consume me I can almost taste it. But I realize the movement of my tongue only means hate has already found place in me. What I see through my windows is merely a reflection. It circles faster than meaning, faster than I can blink my eyes. Plagued by the heat of my blood I bottled the thickness of red, bleached my walls white and made these empty bricks my canvas. With each line brushed against my canvas the growling was now heard from within me. Knowingly I rumble into corruption, acknowledging my fate, my words start to play melody with song my ears never privileged to hear. Words I may have spoken in sleep, but in truth hate has written this harmony and I have created these lyrics.

Daylight

It's the aftereffects of a fall, a trembling earth around my body. No one knows the light can hold the deepest darkness behind its gold. I'VE covered my face with images of hope, considered myself lucky to remember what that looks like. But it held no fortunate purpose. Longing for a settled beat of heart, I shortened my steps and opened my eyes to my surroundings. With no path left to follow I lead myself through stone and gravel, I have fallen many times to find my way, my knees now scrapped and palms raw and bloody. Stone and dirt seep into the skin, it looks as if I've become a part of the earth. Still searching, I struggle along, still waiting. I stamp my blood into the ground, until daylight I wait.

The Invisible Ink

I'VE grazed the day, realization on my motives became brittle, safety seemed cornered to where my decisions in past and present time had seemed like a painting I saw once. Could it have been a book I wrote from blood of the heart, or a sound I can't remember how to harmonize. Am I stronger today? Can I walk away in silent peace? Am I capable of letting go of the chain that bounded me? Set in stone I saw it. Is it fading? Stone can be broken, tears can dry, and time can consider me worthy of mending. I can forget your face, write your name with an old pen, and watch the black ink absorb the genius once upon a time I loved written in the curves of your signature.

Language Portrait

Feeling like a storm that became from the sun. A spear pierced into my heart with icy thorns and body of fire offered nothing from the fire, but given all that can be taken from the ice. My eyes speak in no language, they tell no story to those who can't see behind the flesh. In spirit I am worthy, in darkness I can hide…with words I can shape into portraits for you. Bold red colors and beautiful details in every stroke of my brush of tongue…ask me, and I can show you things you've never seen, take you far away with no change of where you stand. You will see the crumbling of body and chains of a soul. Hold on tight. Don't let go.

Candle in the Dark

My ongoing tolerance for many things have weighed the world on my shoulders. Is it really much to ask of my life to undergo the clarity of peace in need? I have reached into far and unforgiving love. I have dreamt of the simplicity of kindness to be blanketed on my skin. I am built to last, yes, but I am no longer stronger, just hanging on to strength. Hope gathers my bones to withstand the blow I'VE seen rushing toward me, with choice not lying beside me I've led astray to fight. I touch my face and remember my skin. I lick my lips and remember taste. I dry my eyes and forget to cry. It is concrete, solid compromise for hope.

A Book Written by the Blank

Love stories written every day and admired by the lonely. Empty space being filled with fantasy and the aches for more. Familiar pain mixing with the music of the unknown, the uncertain soul begins to wither away in fable lands of story. Simple how often falling off character seems to remind me of where I really sleep. No faraway land nor moment of glory has painted me a different portrait to lay my eyes upon today. I sleep in wonder. I wake in anxiousness for change in the wind, a different current, a stronger gust to carry me where fate wrote its short story.

Doors Shut Windows Open

Although it seems cold, the winters are always more still than summer. The wind blows hard some nights and act as if it carries some sort of treasure to unlock. My window fogs up, but I still try and see through. My eyes still try and see past all the cold. There's always a thought of where I'm looking from, how far am I really? My body has many doorways, and they all seemed to be closed, not locked just closed. Maybe they're not visible or there isn't an easy path to lead here. Who knows what's best for my own invites? There's always an outcome, always a way out, and always a way in.

About the Author

Lucy was inspired to write this book because writing poetry saved her life. Lucy was born and raised in Brooklyn, New York, and within her own childhood tragedies, she started writing journals. Her diaries became her therapy and helped her heal. As Lucy wrote, she became drawn to it. She used her own experiences in her life to paint pictures within her words that for Lucy was a passage to her subconscious. As she got older, her poetry became mature, and others found comfort in her words. With that, Lucy wanted to give the same to whomever may find peace in her poetry.

CPSIA information can be obtained
at www.ICGtesting.com
Printed in the USA
BVHW071241020821
613410BV00006B/163